1

CU00840203

A Place At The Tak
A new model of inclusion of
persons with disabilities into
faith communities.
2nd Edition, Revised

By Brian D. Barber, M.A. Dcn.

Dedication:
For Beth, Emma and Luke, who heard "Can it wait, I'm writing?" entirely too often.

Contents

Forward.

This book is intended as an intoduction to the mechanics of running a church program for persons with intellectual disabilities and autism spectrum disorders. As an introduction, it doesn't suppose to be a complete and exhaustive treatment of the subject. It's intended to point you in what I feel is the right direction. That direction being person centered and concerned with the spiritual lives of people with intellectual disabilities.

The book consists of a few, mercifully brief, sections discussing some of the relevant aspects of what goes into the theoretical basis for a program. This matters because it is better to have a core philosophy at the heart of your program that guides your planning and decision making process. It helps keep things on an even keel. The original audience was not exclusively a Christian audience and so a lot of the language has a clinical and neutral feel. I left a lot of that language in the book because being, well, clinical, is helpful in persuading people that might be on the fence about the practicality of beginning this kind of program.

For example, the discussions of science and psychology and such are intended to give the reader some backgroud information, but also to sort of frame the discussion about what's possible. The 'take home message' of those sections is that we don't know what people can learn and achieve until we try. One of the objections I have heard over the years is that people with intellectual disabilities are not capable of the sort of inner intellectual and spiritual life we accosicate with religious fatih and practice.

To the degree that what we know about intellectual disibilities and cognition speaks to this point at all, it suggests the opposite. There's no good reason for a congregation not to engage and include people with intellectual disibilities so those sections hopefully give the rader a sense of empowerment as they being the process. You've got this.

How this book happened.

This book originally came about as a project for a parish where I was on staff. It sort of took on a life of it's own.

It was accepted for publication in a modified form by an academic journal which resulted in a months long exchange I have described elsewhere as polite but maddening.

So it languished for a while, a victim of the cutting and pasting required for it's former home. If by some bizarre coincidence you happened to get a copy of the book in that form, email me, I'll send you a new one. Or take you to lunch. Or Something.

Circumstances have aligned to make me revisit it. I still work full time with persons on the autism spectrum and am as passionate about reaching them for Christ as ever. I've learned a lot about how to write since this book but i decided to change relatively little of the original text. The facts haven't changed and the intent remains the same: I want you to get passionate about serving this population too. And a little prose goes a long way when you're goal is to let people know they are capable of achieving great things. Since I first wrote this, a lot of the ideas I am advocating have become more mainsteam. This is wonderful, but I decided to leave the original framing more or less intact for the simple reason that I've had the experience of explaining a lot of these issues to people who have either no information or have picked up bad information along the way. So with that in mind, I decided to leave in a lot of material that probably is either common knowledge or self evident to a lot of readers with experience in the field. It might prove useful to you if you need to have some ammunnition if you need to convince a church board or maybe a foundation that offers grants. I sincerely hope it's of use one way or another.

Finally I hope this little book gives you encouragement and confidence to go out and serve the Lord.

Preface: By way of a beginning; an explanation of the problem.

What can the domains of sociology, education and psychology and ethics teach us about how persons with Developmental Disabilities (hereafter abbreviated DD) enter into and function within voluntary communities, especially faith communities?

The answers to this question provides a "best practice" for developing pathways to inclusion for persons with DD into such communities. It is my intention to develop evidence for a best practice model for understanding how to support persons with DD in the process in joining voluntary communities and how to facilitate full and meaningful inclusion.

My interest in this topic was kindled when I was asked by the clergy of a church at which I was on staff to develop some materials for use in both providing religious education to persons with DD. Said materials were then to be used in the ritual practice of our faith tradition so as to be inclusive of this population to the greatest extent possible.

I responded that the idea was a noble one but it had to be done in a way that did not result in a "dumbing-down" of the faith tradition or in an infantilizing of the persons with DD. I proposed a third way, one that in which the message of inclusion was intertwined with and indistinguishable from the medium of inclusion. Educational theorists and others give a lot of time and attention to the concept of inclusion in order to facilitate instruction. In one sense I am examining the facilitation of instruction in order to promote inclusion.

Put another way: What can educational theory, sociology, psychology and ethics tell us about how to truly and meaningfully include persons with developmental disabilities into voluntary communities, in this case, a faith community?

Voluntary association is as natural and necessary a human need as food and water. People may self select to group themselves based on any number of criteria; political belief, ethnicity, shared interest and so on. One of the most common voluntary associations is based on religious identity. This is especially true in this in the U.S., with its rich and varied religious traditions, and absence of a state religion.

For the purpose of this book the faith community will be used as an example of a voluntary community, that is, a community which people choose to belong to and which they are free to enter or leave at will. However, I believe that the lessons learned from this example are applicable to a wide spectrum of voluntary communities. In addition, I intend to use the faith community example because they are typically more narrative driven than, say, the local stamp collector's club.

This is relevant to my thesis because, as I will articulate below, I intend to demonstrate that a narrative driven approach to inclusion for persons with DD is the best practice.

Also, I intend to use this example because it is an excellent place to examine the meeting point between initiation and community. Typically, the person standing outside the voluntary community gains a place inside the voluntary community through adherence to the group idea-set. For example, if one wants to join a Church, Synagogue, or Mosque, there is, at a minimum, a level of adherence to the idea-set of the community which is regarded as a prerequisite.

I am in no way suggesting that voluntary communities (henceforth they will be termed faith communities) need to do away with this model as these communities have every right to define and defend that which they believe to be true. I am suggesting that, especially for persons with DD, the underlying narrative informing the idea-set, and the individual's place within that narrative, is a more appropriate basis for inclusion than the ability to pontificate on the arcane details of the idea-set extrapolated from the narrative.

I believe that the current best practice on diversity in education has a lot to say to this process. Much of that work is built around the idea that inclusion is a function of language as much as anything else. With that in mind, I will outline a proposal for an inclusion model that is "narrative based" as opposed to the "construct based" model that I believe predominates the field currently.

Further, I intend to demonstrate that this is the direction in which the best research and practice leads us. I intend to review the literature to develop a picture of the best practices in inclusion of persons with Developmental Disabilities and demonstrate how that best practice can be applied to inclusion to voluntary communities.

As I mentioned above, I have been asked to develop an inclusion model for use by local churches and this work will be further developed for eventual implementation as a program for providing a faith community experience for persons with developmental disabilities.

That is, the hypothetical model I describe will be put into practice in the near future. I have already been humbled to discover that the interest in my work is considerable among both professionals in the developmental disabilities field and those interested in the social and religious implications of my work. I have spoken to educational and mental health professionals from a variety of faith traditions that are interested in my thesis and wish to use some of the work I have already developed in their own programs. As recently as the date this passage was written, I have been approached by non-profit agencies that have become aware of my work and have asked me to consult on their interactions with persons with developmental disabilities.

There has already been a considerable amount of work done on how to include persons with Developmental disabilities into faith communities. However, as my research will show, most of that work has been done in addressing the narrow question of modification of educational materials to accommodate disability in order to facilitate a specific act of inclusion (typically in the Christian traditions this would mean confirmation or first communion, or in some Protestant traditions, baptism) and having a limited scope beyond the rite of inclusion for which the inclusion/ educational model was developed.

The model I have developed takes a more holistic approach in that it moves beyond mere education on the one hand and beyond the initial act of inclusion on the other. My work is based in large measure on what the discipline of sociology can tell us about how people (both disabled and not) enter into communities.

In all of the models I have encountered, the educational component is paramount. In mine, it is present but within and subordinate to, the overall context of inclusion as both a process and a goal. Further, my work is based on the idea that inclusion is narrative driven, which is, as far as I can tell, unique in the academic considerations of this issue. I believe this topic is important (especially at this time) for several reasons.

First, as state budgets shrink, more and more people are turning to nongovernmental organizations for support and assistance. It is vital that religious organizations have an understanding of the developmentally disabled population that reflects a best practice and that would be considered appropriate and viable even from a secular perspective. That is, the question of best practice in inclusion transcends questions of faith. A best practice model should meet objective standards regardless of its application.

Lastly, we have had nearly a generation of inclusion in the public schools and in most areas of life. I believe the time is ripe for inclusion models in faith communities that are broader and fuller than previous models. The mainstreaming of persons with developmental disabilities has been commonplace for long enough that the public prejudice against persons with DD is at its lowest point perhaps ever.

However this is not to say all is well. I have encountered a considerable dissatisfaction among persons with DD and their advocates with the current available programs. The greater part of these dissatisfactions are articulated throughout this paper, but they include a perceived lack of interest in responding to the concerns of the DD population, the "othering" of persons with DD and often, unfair and irrational beliefs about the DD population held my community members. I believe that now, for the reasons stated above, is the right time to address their concerns.

Most of my work is going to be based on existing research in the sociological and education study of developmental disabilities. It is in effect, a synthesis of existing work into a new and novel model. My first step has been to familiarize myself with the existing work in these fields. I have also interviewed persons working in existing programs which parallel the model I am developing. I have attended educational workshops offered by developmental disabilities educators of other faith traditions.

I intend to outline the current state of the art in the field, outline the current sociological research which has (as is central to my thesis) not been fully considered by the developers of current inclusion models and to articulate a new model for inclusion and to provide examples of how the new inclusion model might be implemented through sample educational and ritual models based on the research.

For the greater part, I will be referencing well established research in the developmental disabilities and sociological fields. In very limited cases, I will refer to interviews I have conducted with professionals in the fields relevant to the thesis. I have obtained the materials I am using from public libraries and from research libraries to which I pay membership dues. Some of the material I use has originated at seminars on the topic I have taken and from other meetings and workshops relevant to my thesis.

1. A place at the table What difference does difference make?

This is the perennial question at the heart of any discussion in the MR/DD community. The less often spoken corollary is: What can be done to minimize difference in a real and meaningful way? In a sense this paper in an attempt to offer an affirmative answer in at least one sphere of life. The hypothesis underlying this thesis is this: Difference becomes manifest in community- that is, for a person to be different than the others in a group of persons, there must be a group of persons to be different from and to which a comparative relationship exists. This "normative" group must have some characteristics of sameness from which the "other" deviates in some manner.

In most cases (beyond mere physical appearance) this involves a sense of sameness based on shared ideas and values. Ideas and values are in many respects a function of language. The use of language (especially as applied to the self identity of groups) almost always functions in the context of narrative. The narrative defines the group which defines the position of persons within or outside of the group.

We often use the term "othering" to describe NOT being included in a group or community. Usually this term is applied to race, gender, ethnicity, etc. But we do not often apply these modes of thinking to the opposite, the "we-ing" as it were of persons, particularly the disabled. I believe that inclusion begins at the narrative.

The stories we tell ourselves about ourselves matter. They matter most in the places in which we WANT to be part of the narrative, such as a faith community. This observation does little to actually maximize the person's engagement and involvement. So, what does the practical application of this thesis look like? One truth must be that there is inevitably going to be some difference between "maximum possible inclusion" and ''full inclusion" into the daily life of a faith community.

This is painful but real. I realize that some people may even take umbrage at my presupposing this. However, for a variety of reasons, not the least of which is that I have an opportunity to actually field test my ideas upon completion of this book, I believe the real goal must be to develop real life inclusion models, not to indulge in political correctness run amok.

I believe that the best possible outcomes can be found in models of religious instruction and public observance that are narrative driven and make full use of the current state of the art in the educational and sociological disciplines. It's also the case that a best practice for inclusion is one that is validated by both the faith tradition and by secular disciplines. That is, all parties observing a narrative driven inclusion model should be able to observe within it a genuine respect for both the institution and the individual.

A successful model is one in which the model works to the good of all. One in which the person with DD is neither a token nor a drain, but one in which the person blesses the community with their presence and in turn is blessed by being present.

2. A few thoughts on populations: MR/DD terms and descriptions.

What do the terms used in this book actually mean? As a practical matter, the generally accepted definition of Developmental Disability is, essentially, testing at an IQ of 70 or below on an accepted test. What does this mean? It can mean any number of things. It usually means there is present within the person's cognitive makeup deficits in speech and language processing, problem solving, and educational development.

Persons in this category may present as emotionally immature or unable to handle adult responsibilities. Psychologists frequently speak of the "mental age" or "emotional age" of a person as being substantially below their chronological age. As a rule, persons with DD fall below the baseline understood as denoting an "adult." (Florian) One way to understand the implications of this is to realize that to quote Mark Rapley "…. some people do, it appears, require a substantial degree of assistance with managing the affairs of everyday life." (Rapley)

This is a reality beyond the massaging of any social construction. Is this problematic for religious inclusion? No it is not. Virtually every religious tradition recognizes a place for persons who have assumed full inclusion in the responsibilities of the faith but have not yet assumed the full responsibilities of adulthood. The term "age of reason" or some corollary is frequently used to denote such a point in development. For the purpose of this book it will be assumed that the persons with a DD described in this paper (unless otherwise noted) have a developmental baseline equal to or greater than the "age of reason" described by most of the world's faiths.

Again, as a practical matter, this would mean a "mental age" of around 9-13 years old give or take a year or so either way depending on the tradition. I realize that is a broad range but I want to be inclusive of both faith traditions and persons with DD to the greatest extent possible within the scope of this work. Also, I want to be very careful to avoid taking sides, as it were, in affirming one tradition's conception of the age of reason over another, so I have erred on the side of being merely descriptive.

Who are the persons who would be served by this model most directly?

The breadth of the spectrum of persons with developmental disabilities is substantial. If for no other reason than the fact that at some point I will have to end this book, I will begin with a few operational assumptions that, while they may seem arbitrary, are essentially the ones used in the research my work is based upon.

The severely and profoundly disabled, those who for whatever reason are unable to communicate meaningfully, are beyond the scope of this book. Likewise, this book does not make any specific recommendations on addressing modification of extreme behaviors, the "dual diagnosed" person, or other categories of persons whose circumstances are best addressed in the medical literature.

Broadly speaking, the people my work is primarily concerned with are those in the mild to moderate spectrum of developmental disability. That is, persons who have full use of speech (including those with impediments, limited vocabulary, etc), self awareness, and ability to discern as sense of the sacred (I realize that the last is highly subjective). Some commentators have posited that this translates to a minimum "mental age" of about 6 years of age.

That may be too arbitrary, but I would say that some indication of a desire to participate in the life of a faith community qua faith community is essential. For example, for participation in the life of a faith community to have meaning, there must be some sense of what might be termed the "metaphysical other," the thing outside of oneself or apart from the immediate physical reality, that is being connected with. Since my personal belief is that this is innate in the human spirit I would be very open to participation by any and all who showed any interest or desire to be included in such a community.

The primary reason for limiting the scope of this thesis is that we run into the issue of voluntary participation. It is extremely important that people freely choose to join or not to join a faith community with no hint or anything that smacks of coercion. Even something as subtle as the fact that ones' friends or housemates are "doing it" may be problematic. The issues of peer and authority figure pressure are (generally) outside the scope of this book, and will only be addressed in passing.

For the purposes of this book I am going to assume sincere, voluntary, interest on the part of the individual. To do otherwise would, at the very least, create a Sargasso Sea of grammar and syntax issues in the body of the work. I don't want to qualify every sentence in this book.

One final thought by way of introduction. I will describe and at times "pick apart" the work of others who have labored in these fields. Whatever my academic observations of the attempts of others to build a bridge between the developmentally disabled and God as understood within their respective faith traditions, I have nothing but unfettered admiration for all who have sought to show love to those most often thought incapable of understanding it.

One other note: I am aware that much of the language in this book reflects a Judeo-Christian outlook. This is mainly a reflection of the research upon which the book is based and in no way intended as bias against other traditions.

The handbook at the back of the book is written explicitly from a Christian viewpoint to demonstrate the application of the idea of the book in a "real life" setting. It is my sincere hope that persons of faith would use the information and ideas contained to bless those whom they serve regardless of creed.

3. A discussion of "truth Sets" and their application to this book.

Does this book intend to describe any theological or metaphysical truth? The simple answer is, "no." This book is not about religion in the sense of making a case for the superiority of one faith tradition over another. It is a call to what, almost without exception, all faith communities articulate as their highest ideals: Inclusion in the narrative for all who desire it.

So what does it mean to be a member of a faith community and developmentally disabled? What should it mean? Simply stated, at its irreducible core, inclusion in a faith community for a person with DD means that the meta-narrative of the group applies equally to the individual with DD as to any other member of the group. It would be easy to suggest that this is implied or self evident in most traditions.

On some level, I might agree that it at least ought to be. However, most traditions have what might be termed an education of initiation that "makes" a member of the community. Examples include Catechism class or Hebrew school. (Diaz)

Many faith traditions offer alternative curriculum for persons with DD that prepares the person for one or more specific rites or ceremonies.

All too frequently, these approaches, (with good intentions) frequently "drag the person across the goal line", and in effect, leave them there. That is, there is no real effect of the initiation on the person. If anything, it could be argued that whatever benefit there is, is accrued by the group by having given itself permission to feel good about its tolerance and high-mindedness.

I will describe a variety of approaches to religious instruction and inclusion, but it is not my intent to describe the faith traditions which utilize any or all of these methods as superior or inferior to one another. I explicitly deny any suggestion that a critique of an inclusion model is a critique of the tradition using it. In point of candor, I find considerable fault with some of the inclusion models used by my own faith tradition.

Furthermore, I will explicitly not address the larger question of the validity of metaphysics. Since the basis of this thesis question is: How can information gleaned from a variety of disciplines used to address the idea of inclusion within a faith tradition? The inherent validity of the faith community is both implied and irrelevant. In one sense, it is sort of the point of this book; that whether or not you believe in a god or in the existence of a particular God, there are some evidence based practices for the inclusion of persons with DD into voluntary faith based communities that are valid on their face. It is these things that are the topic of this book. It is of great importance that a person who had no interest in the underlying metaphysics be able to review these models and affirm them as evidence based practice.

The educational perspective concerning the engagement, instruction and socialization of persons with disabilities: a starting point for examining the data.

When people talk about inclusion what do they in fact, mean? There are many possible answers but the models found in the context of education are the most common. They also serve as the presuppositions for most of the programs and models of inclusion used in religious instruction.

Typically, what has happened is that the ideas in current usage about how to include persons with DD into a classroom are as it were, cut and pasted, into the realm of religious instruction.

A typical model of classroom inclusion would be something on the order of this list of steps of inclusion outlined by Luftig as follows.

5 basic steps of inclusion:
"1. Know what inclusion means

2. Know why inclusion is important.

3. Know what the goals are.

4. Know how to build a program in typical environments.

5. Know how to help children make friends."

There is much to be gained in internalizing these ideas as values. But it is worth considering that the idea of building a program in a 'typical environment" is paramount in this model. Classroom inclusion herein is about goals and results, the sort of thing that might be termed "endgame."

This is reasonable since the classroom is about results -either you learn or you do not- in a way that, I submit, religious inclusion is not. Notice that in the above paragraph, the term religious inclusion, not religious instruction was used. It is easy to confuse the term because for so many of us, our experience of education was our experience of inclusion. It may have been a baptism or catechism class or Hebrew classes pursuant to a Bar/Bat Mitzvah or any number of possibilities.

The idea that learning a set of facts and being able to be conversant in them denotes status in a community is (as noted above) almost universal.

But this begs an important question: Is it necessary that a limited ability to articulate the nuances of a tradition inherently mean limited access to and inclusion within that tradition? The reflexive answer is of course "no" insofar as my thesis assumes inclusion as a positive good. It is worth pointing out that the idea of a correlation between articulation of ideas and inclusion in a community is tied to notions of privileging education to a degree that we have only done in our society for the last few generations.

We will discuss the social construction of disability in other parts of this book, but suffice it to say, DD can be seen as relative to the overall intellectual life of the community in which the person is participating.

Educators have, for example, long observed the phenomenon sometimes called "3 o'clock retardation" (Rapley) in which a student is placed in special education, functions academically within the DD spectrum but upon leaving school (that is, at 3 o'clock) functions normally with their peers. Intellectual disability does not inherently mean social disability.

Put another way, there is no objective reason why DD has to

mean a diminished status or valuation within a community or even a diminished role. It very well might in some cases, perhaps even in many cases, but the presupposition that it is simply incorrect. Besides being factually incorrect, it is morally objectionable to assume that DD ought to automatically exclude people from participation in any area of life.

With this in mind, we can consider the above steps to inclusion. There are of course other notions of inclusion but this list is both generally inclusive of the current ideas and broad enough to develop generalities from. Beginning with "know what inclusion means" we immediately see some of the obstacles to transposing the academic constructs of inclusion to the realm of faith communities.

Inclusion for a classroom may be (relatively) self explanatory. But is inclusion for a person with DD in say, a Quaker unprogrammed meeting the same as inclusion in an Orthodox Shabbat? Is inclusion in a fundamentalist Baptist revival meeting the same as inclusion in a Roman Catholic mass? The practical technical details in each of these cases would of course appear different to an outside observer, but I would submit that the answer to our question is "yes." It is "yes" to the extent that the person is included in the narrative that the ritual activity reinforces.

The "nuts and bolts" of inclusion within the ritual observance give the person meaning within the community in the same way that the person gives the various facets of ritual meaning. To know what inclusion means in a faith community is to experience an understanding that "I belong here, I am not an outsider."

This matters on several levels. Not the least of which is that many well meaning attempts to provide faith community reinforce the idea of persons with DD as outsiders. For example, one faith community I observed, which I am reluctant to single out, referred to persons with DD as "our special friends." When we deconstruct the phrase we can see that "our" refers to the primary group, "special" is self evident but denotes an "other" by its nature, and "friends" implies that the DD are guests, not members of the group.

No matter how well intentioned the people running such a program, the construction of the idea set at the heart of the work undermined the whole. The second item in our outline is "know why inclusion is important." It is fair to consider a variety of reasons for inclusion. The most commonly voiced is perhaps the idea that the faith community is central to the life of the natural supports of the person with DD and that inclusion in the community is a natural extension of inclusion in the family.

Most religious groups would hold that inclusion is important by virtue of the inherent value of the individual with DD. Irrespective of theological differences; we could describe this as a valuation of the "soul" of the individual apart from any identification with the individual person with DD. This may become problematic in the sense that inclusion could become a "duty" on the part of the institution and runs the risk of being seen as an onerous obligation. This is an outcome no one would desire.

However, this leads us to the next point which is to 'know what the goals are." This begs the question: are the "goals" of inclusion the same for all groups? In many superficial respects they are clearly not the same. I would submit that an approach that states that placing the person with DD (or for that matter all persons) within the meta-narrative of the group is the goal of inclusion regardless of the nuances of any particular faith tradition. "Typical environments" is one of those phrases that demonstrate the difference between the classroom and the faith community. We could easily make a parallel between a classroom and, say, a Sunday school class or a church service.

There are some legitimate parallels in that the institutions that oversee both expect the experiences to produce some level of conformity and there is an expectation of decorum in both and so on. However, it may be useful to broaden our notions of how a faith community operates to get a better understanding of the topic.

Any activity or setting that is seen by the group as reinforcing the ethos of the group can be seen as a "typical environment." This may be perceived by some as a side issue and an attempt to strain at gnats, but if the notion of what "space" persons with DD are allowed to occupy is not addressed, then this whole exercise becomes nothing more than yet another way to "trot out" the DD in a setting convenient to the larger community, put them through their paces so as to make other people feel better about themselves, and be done with them for another week.

The necessity of 'set aside space' in a school or other institution is reasonable enough to the extent that institution exists to serve an external reality. Schools exist to provide education; hospitals exist to provide medical care, and so on. Ideally, a faith community would not describe any of its activities (worship services, or other group events) as "off limits" to the DD population.

More importantly, faith communities should strive not to allow tacit understandings to form about access. All of this is to say that there ought not to be any "typical environments" for the DD person in a faith community; at least not in a restrictive sense. But it is also to remind us that a faith community lives together as well as prays together.

It is not just enough to create a safe and inviting space for the use of persons with DD in public worship (which is central to this thesis) it is also important to conceptualize inclusion as "happening" in other areas such as at social events, like group meals and holiday celebrations.

A new model for conceptualizing inclusion in the ritual life of a community and in the educational foundations of a community must be translatable to the daily life of the community. The final bullet point of this list is "Know how to help children make friends." This is a perfectly laudable goal in school or without. The core value here could be described as "socialization." It is worth noting here that the ultimate onus to "make friends" is on the child, or, in this case, the person with DD. This is exactly as it should be. Faith communities can be welcoming, and inclusive. They can be as up to date and politically correct as they desire. But at the end of the day, the extent to which a person is included in a group is a choice.

An inclusive faith community should be a safe and welcoming environment, and I doubt anyone would disagree with that. But it is vital that the interpersonal relationships facilitated by whatever model of inclusion is being utilized be real in every sense, and not an empty gesture or a learned behavior. We should be aware and supportive of how to help people with DD "make friends" and engage socially to whatever degree possible.

But, having created this space, it is incumbent on the leadership of the community to allow (within self evident limits) all persons, especially those with DD, to form such personal relationships as they will and to allow those relationships to rise or fall on their own merits.

Another way of saying this is that a healthy model of inclusion is one where the community has gotten past any notions of fake or superficial politeness or friendliness. The point of this exercise is to show that merely laying the ideas of Special Education on top of one faith communities' traditions or another's is bound to make matters worse. Anyone who ever relished the prospect of a snow day off from school knows that no matter how beneficial it may be for us, school was something that was done TO us not BY us at least until be got old enough to start paying for it. This is often how religious inclusion has been socially constructed for many of us as well. And it is this mindset we would do well to exercise from our thinking about the inclusion of person's with DD into any community especially a faith community. An institution such as a school is engaging with the person in order to discharge an obligation, a faith community fails when it acts likewise.

The educational model and inclusion:

For the most part, the vast majority of inclusion models used throughout a wide variety of faith traditions have their basis in the field of special education. This is understandable. The simple truth is that for many years the special education field was the only place where persons with DD were taken seriously as persons. However, over the last few years, a wide spectrum of work has been done on DD in the field of sociology and in the social construction of disability.

It is prudent to consider what the social sciences have to teach us about DD and community inclusion. In essence, most of the programs used to "teach" inclusion follow a preset pattern. The central ideas of the faith tradition are distilled into teachable and repeatable pieces of information in order to facilitate their regurgitation. While I can understand any number of critiques of this method, the underlying idea set is valid insofar as any tradition had the right to define itself. It is also how we "teach" religion in the secular world.

A freshman college student in a World religions' class doesn't learn about what it "means" to be Jewish or Christian or Hindu. He learns the 5 pillars of Islam and the Eightfold Path of the Buddha, and the 10 Commandments and so on.

I mention this because I want to reiterate that I am not opposed to idea sets or even composing identity based upon them. I am merely concerned with "context" for the purposes of this book.

Most educational models for instruction and inclusion (we could also use the word "mainstreaming") use a paradigm that looks similar to the one below.

In "Positive Behavioral Support: Including People with Difficult Behavior in the Community", Koegel and Dunlap offer the following model.

They write:

"Specific behaviors for PAC Development:

1. Learning outcomes are identified; the knowledge acquired by the students

2. Possible alternatives for presentation are identified and considered for use; for example taped textbook.

3. Available materials and equipment are Identified for possible use.

4. Students are evaluated for learning style, learning preference

and/or achievement level.

5. Alternatives for presentation (i.e. taped books, discussion methods) are decided upon and matched with student learning styles or preferences.

6. Software materials are developed for future use (i.e. slides are collected, transparencies are made, or textbooks are taped.)

7. Presentation is implemented

8. Student progress is evaluated in a traditional and/or alternative manner such as oral or multiple choice tests."

Later Developments.

However, over the last few years, a wide spectrum of work has been done on DD in the field of sociology and in the social construction of disability. It is prudent to consider what the social sciences have to teach us about DD and community inclusion.

In essence, most of the programs used to "teach" inclusion follow a preset pattern. The central ideas of the faith tradition are distilled into teachable and repeatable pieces of information in order to facilitate their regurgitation.

To change the model we have to change the way people think about the role of DD in the life of the person with DD.

Shakespeare and Watson write:

"To assume that disability will always be the key to (their) identity is to recapitulate the error made by those from the medical model perspective who define people by their impairment. Any individual disabled person may strategically identify, at different times as a person with a particular gender, ethnicity, sexuality, occupation, religion, or football team. Identity cannot be straightforwardly read off any more; it is, within limit, a matter of choice."

This is especially true when looking at the language used in ritual and public observance by this group. What is remarkable about this is that it places the person inside the underlying narrative of the tradition. It makes, "internalizing the story" of equal status with "articulating the fact-set."

Most religious education is based on absorbing and retaining idea sets. Whether this is some form of Catechesis or "bible study" or by some other name, the core concept is that one's place in the group is defined and validated by being able to absorb, retain, and regurgitate the truth set of the tradition.

The question that sadly arises is often: Is it possible for "those people" to understand what they are hearing? The evidence suggests that the answer is yes.

Hattum writes: "It appears that mentally retarded and nonretarded individuals do not differ significantly in iconic and echoic memory functioning. Likewise, it appears that modifications or improved functioning in the system cannot occur through training or practice. Thus the perceptual buffers should not be a major concern of special educators."

For the purposes of our discussion, this can be understood to mean that information that is communicated meaningfully is received meaningfully. By meaningful we mean language that is both at a vocabulary level appropriate to the listener and is couched in contexts or schema that is meaningful. To give an example of how that can be experienced we can refer to the following discussion of displacement, which has parallels to the problems faced in developing a new model of inclusion:

Hattum writes:

"Displacement refers to the child's ability to refer to objects not physically present or to events which have occurred in the past or which will occur in the future. The ability to handle displacement is a key component of intelligence. Young children often cannot handle past and future in their language functioning."

In this we see that the problem may be not so much vocabulary but schema; the context of the language, the story itself becomes the carrier of the language, not the language of the story.

4. The educational perspective concerning the engagement, instruction and socialization of persons with disabilities: a starting point for examining the data.

When people talk about inclusion what do they in fact, mean? There are many possible answers but the models found in the context of education are the most common. They also serve as the presuppositions for most of the programs and models of inclusion used in religious instruction.

Typically, what has happened is that the ideas in current usage about how to include persons with DD into a classroom are as it were, cut and pasted, into the realm of religious instruction.

A typical model of classroom inclusion would be something on the order of this list of steps of inclusion outlined by Luftig as follows

5 basic steps of inclusion:
"1. Know what inclusion means

2. Know why inclusion is important.

3. Know what the goals are.

4. Know how to build a program in typical environments.

5. Know how to help children make friends."

There is much to be gained in internalizing these ideas as values. But it is worth considering that the idea of building a program in a 'typical environment" is paramount in this model. Classroom inclusion herein is about goals and results, the sort of thing that might be termed "endgame."

This is reasonable since the classroom is about results -either you learn or you do not- in a way that, I submit, religious inclusion is not. Notice that in the above paragraph, the term religious inclusion, not religious instruction was used. It is easy to confuse the term because for so many of us, our experience of education was our experience of inclusion. It may have been a baptism or catechism class or Hebrew classes pursuant to a Bar/Bat Mitzvah or any number of possibilities. The idea that learning a set of facts and being able to be conversant in them denotes status in a community is (as noted above) almost universal.

But this begs an important question: Is it necessary that a limited ability to articulate the nuances of a tradition inherently mean limited access to and inclusion within that tradition? The reflexive answer is of course "no" insofar as my thesis assumes inclusion as a positive good. It is worth pointing out that the idea of a correlation between articulation of ideas and inclusion in a community is tied to notions of privileging education to a degree that we have only done in our society for the last few generations. We will discuss the social construction of disability in other parts of this book, but suffice it to say, DD can be seen as relative to the overall intellectual life of the community in which the person is participating.

Educators have, for example, long observed the phenomenon sometimes called "3 o'clock retardation" (Rapley) in which a student is placed in special education, functions academically within the DD spectrum but upon leaving school (that is, at 3 o'clock) functions normally with their peers. Intellectual disability does not inherently mean social disability.

Put another way, there is no objective reason why DD has to mean a diminished status or valuation within a community or even a diminished role. It very well might in some cases, perhaps even in many cases, but the presupposition that it is simply incorrect. Besides being factually incorrect, it is morally objectionable to assume that DD ought to automatically exclude people from participation in any area of life.

With this in mind, we can consider the above steps to inclusion. There are of course other notions of inclusion but this list is both generally inclusive of the current ideas and broad enough to develop generalities from. Beginning with "know what inclusion means" we immediately see some of the obstacles to transposing the academic constructs of inclusion to the realm of faith communities.

Inclusion for a classroom may be (relatively) self explanatory. But is inclusion for a person with DD in say, a Quaker unprogrammed meeting the same as inclusion in an Orthodox Shabbat? Is inclusion in a fundamentalist Baptist revival meeting the same as inclusion in a Roman Catholic mass? The practical technical details in each of these cases would of course appear different to an outside observer, but I would submit that the answer to our question is "yes." It is "yes" to the extent that the person is included in the narrative that the ritual activity reinforces.

The "nuts and bolts" of inclusion within the ritual observance give the person meaning within the community in the same way that the person gives the various facets of ritual meaning. To know what inclusion means in a faith community is to experience an understanding that "I belong here, I am not an outsider."

This matters on several levels. Not the least of which is that many well meaning attempts to provide faith community reinforce the idea of persons with DD as outsiders. For example, one faith community I observed, which I am reluctant to single out, referred to persons with DD as "our special friends." When we deconstruct the phrase we can see that "our" refers to the primary group, "special" is self evident but denotes an "other" by its nature, and "friends" implies that the DD are guests, not members of the group.

No matter how well intentioned the people running such a program, the construction of the idea set at the heart of the work undermined the whole. The second item in our outline is "know why inclusion is important." It is fair to consider a variety of reasons for inclusion. The most commonly voiced is perhaps the idea that the faith community is central to the life of the natural supports of the person with DD and that inclusion in the community is a natural extension of inclusion in the family.

Most religious groups would hold that inclusion is important by virtue of the inherent value of the individual with DD. Irrespective of theological differences; we could describe this as a valuation of the "soul" of the individual apart from any identification with the individual person with DD. This may become problematic in the sense that inclusion could become a "duty" on the part of the institution and runs the risk of being seen as an onerous obligation. This is an outcome no one would desire.

However, this leads us to the next point which is to 'know what the goals are." This begs the question: are the "goals" of inclusion the same for all groups? In many superficial respects they are clearly not the same. I would submit that an approach that states that placing the person with DD (or for that matter all persons) within the meta-narrative of the group is the goal of inclusion regardless of the nuances of any particular faith tradition. "Typical environments" is one of those phrases that demonstrate the difference between the classroom and the faith community. We could easily make a parallel between a classroom and, say, a Sunday school class or a church service.

There are some legitimate parallels in that the institutions that oversee both expect the experiences to produce some level of conformity and there is an expectation of decorum in both and so on. However, it may be useful to broaden our notions of how a faith community operates to get a better understanding of the topic.

Any activity or setting that is seen by the group as reinforcing the ethos of the group can be seen as a "typical environment." This may be perceived by some as a side issue and an attempt to strain at gnats, but if the notion of what "space" persons with DD are allowed to occupy is not addressed, then this whole exercise becomes nothing more than yet another way to "trot out" the DD in a setting convenient to the larger community, put them through their paces so as to make other people feel better about themselves, and be done with them for another week.

The necessity of 'set aside space' in a school or other institution is reasonable enough to the extent that institution exists to serve an external reality. Schools exist to provide education; hospitals exist to provide medical care, and so on. Ideally, a faith community would not describe any of its activities (worship services, or other group events) as "off limits" to the DD population.

More importantly, faith communities should strive not to allow tacit understandings to form about access. All of this is to say that there ought not to be any "typical environments" for the DD person in a faith community; at least not in a restrictive sense. But it is also to remind us that a faith community lives together as well as prays together. It is not just enough to create a safe and inviting space for the use of persons with DD in public worship (which is central to this thesis) it is also important to conceptualize inclusion as "happening" in other areas such as at social events, like group meals and holiday celebrations.

A new model for conceptualizing inclusion in the ritual life of a community and in the educational foundations of a community must be translatable to the daily life of the community. The final bullet point of this list is "Know how to help children make friends." This is a perfectly laudable goal in school or without. The core value here could be described as "socialization." It is worth noting here that the ultimate onus to "make friends" is on the child, or, in this case, the person with DD. This is exactly as it should be. Faith communities can be welcoming, and inclusive. They can be as up to date and politically correct as they desire. But at the end of the day, the extent to which a person is included in a group is a choice.

An inclusive faith community should be a safe and welcoming environment, and I doubt anyone would disagree with that. But it is vital that the interpersonal relationships facilitated by whatever model of inclusion is being utilized be real in every sense, and not an empty gesture or a learned behavior. We should be aware and supportive of how to help people with DD "make friends" and engage socially to whatever degree possible. But, having created this space, it is incumbent on the leadership of the community to allow (within self evident limits) all persons, especially those with DD, to form such personal relationships as they will and to allow those relationships to rise or fall on their own merits.

Another way of saying this is that a healthy model of inclusion is one where the community has gotten past any notions of fake or superficial politeness or friendliness. The point of this exercise is to show that merely laying the ideas of Special Education on top of one faith communities' traditions or another's is bound to make matters worse. Anyone who ever relished the prospect of a snow day off from school knows that no matter how beneficial it may be for us, school was something that was done TO us not BY us at least until be got old enough to start paying for it. This is often how religious inclusion has been socially constructed for many of us as well.

And it is this mindset we would do well to exercise from our thinking about the inclusion of person's with DD into any community especially a faith community. An institution such as a school is engaging with the person in order to discharge an obligation, a faith community fails when it acts likewise.

5. Education, Linguistics, and the faith tradition's "truth set:

In one sense, it is hard to argue against highly stratified and linear language and for linguistic comprehension being the standard of practice because if religion is not concerned with affirming, and promulgating, a specific idea set, then why does it exist?

The response is that in an age when many of us have become too well educated for our own good it is easy to forget that these faith traditions did not begin as theological propositions, they began as stories. Someone told someone else about Moses or Jesus, or the Buddha or what have you.

This is not in any way a critique of religion or a critique of any particular tradition, but more of an observation of how our minds work. Most of us respond well to information presented in narrative form and have a harder time processing disconnected facts. For example, I would wager I would get a more coherent set of responses from asking a dozen people to describe their wedding than to recite the last 10 phone numbers they dialed.

Insofar as the information presented in religious education is information then it stands to reason that it could be presented as narrative. In fact, it could be argued that at one point all religious instruction and all of the religious activity it resulted in is driven by narrative. The literature of all many of the world's great religions relates and is often mainly concerned with, the tradition's founder telling stories. I would almost go so far as to suggest that a narrative based model of religious instruction and inclusion does not need to be defended but that every other model does.

The sociological perspective: What does a religion "DO" in a sense that can be quantified by neutral observers?

Social scientists observe 3 major functions of religion: Beckford describes them as follows: 3 Major functions of religion:
1. Social cohesion.
2. Social control (cultural and moral norms)
3. Providing meaning and purpose.

It is worth considering these ideas as they apply to persons with DD. What is social cohesion? Typically social scientists would have in mind something like the protector of the status quo that was the medieval Roman Catholic Church or the stabilizing force of Islam over various tribes and factions under a Caliphate. This might be termed Macro-social cohesion. There are other ways of deconstructing social cohesion.

Persons with DD can in fairness be generally assumed to have smaller social networks than average and to be dependant to one degree or another on pre-existing social structures. This is relevant because how we understand "society" can be seen as a construct in its own right.

If a person with DD is included meaningfully within their faith community they are inherently more fully included into the larger culture that community exits within than if they were marginalized from the faith community.

That is, if the community is 'binding' the person to themselves then the community is playing the role of bringing the person with DD into a state-of being within the community and the larger culture. The person now has their individual identity, but is now a member of this or that faith tradition, which in turn functions within a larger culture. The faith becomes a sort of "you are here" sign for the person.

This holds true irrespective of whether or not a person has DD but is especially important in the lives of persons with DD and others for who the "markers" of social cohesion are few. Social cohesion and social control are not the same thing. One is a statement that there is a tribe. The other is a statement that the tribe has rules. The most common mental image associated with the idea of social control is of reactionary forces suppressing some impulse or behavior defined as "sin."

Of course, a great deal of that sort of thing has gone on in human history. But the reality is more complicated. Social control is about context: You may act this way here, but not that way there.

For example, if a surgeon operates on you and sends you a bill, this is not unusual. If however, I cut someone open and take their cash, it is robbery, assault, and any number of other felonies. The difference is an understood social control that people who go to medical school and jump through other hoops can do things in one context that I cannot do in another. It is a social contract taken to one of its many logical conclusions.

Religions do enforce the social contract as part of their function at a macro-level. Religions promote social control by many different routes. The most obvious is the sort of authoritarian rule of a ruling religious class. Examples, from the Medici Popes to the Taliban, abound. Apart from that, religions can use less overt pressures to maintain social norms. In the lives of persons with DD (and I strongly suspect in the lives of most people) the force for social control is not invocation of a wrathful god but the praise and disapproval of one's friends and neighbors.

The instinct for many of us is to bristle at the thought of anyone controlling us, and religion is often slandered as a tyrannical force for control. Could it not be argued though, that in the case of a person with DD, the extent to which a person is self-regulated by virtue of a desire to integrate themselves into the community is evidence of the positive role of religion as a force of social cohesion?

The risks for unwelcome control are stipulated. But it is worth observing here that while the dynamics in the life of a person with DD may be more readily apparent, they are essentially the same as anyone else. Meaning and purpose are words that often run the risk of becoming, like "pretty", "well" and "fine", rendered meaningless through overuse.

The inherent meaning or purpose of any life are far, far, beyond the scope of this book but for the purpose of this discussion we can substitute something like "externally directed self actualization." Concepts like "I belong here" are their own validation. It is unfair and unwise to dig around inside anyone's mind. And, further, I am not in favor of the habit of many professionals and natural supports to dissect the minds of persons with DD on the assumption that they are somehow easily understood. Even if we accept that we can only know others by reporting, if a person with DD reports finding meaning in a faith tradition who are we to say that they are connecting to a baser emotions such as mere overstimulation or the excitement of being in a crowd?

Meaning and purpose are slippery ideas at the best of times and it is best left up to the individual to determine these things for themselves. The only objective external measure of meaning in this context is the extent to which the individual engages the sacred as a result of being included into the larger group. It may be a case of "the medium is the message."

 Consider Beckford:

"…..the sacred is the focus of ritual, which is formal ceremonial behavior….what is sacred, however, we set apart from everyday life."

In this we see that the thing we render as purpose cannot be merely mundane or merely functional. To imagine (in the sense of forming an image in one's mind, not in the sense of 'make believe') a purpose or a meaning is to have a sense of self in relation to the "Other." This construct of a purpose of religion is to provide meaning is understood in both the secular and religious language, albeit with much different terms and idea sets being used on the part of faith traditions.

6. Where are we now? The social construction of developmental disabilities:

What does "social construction" mean: Simply put, it means that our ideas exist in one or more contexts. A proper definition of social construction is as follows from Macionis,

He writes:

"…… the fundamental concepts of any human activity are social constructions. People collectively create the idea with which they grasp the world, and they collectively modify those ideas over time. For example no one encounters "poverty" in the raw; we encounter it through a socially constructed discourse about poverty-a collection of public and private talk that encourages us to think that the topic of our conversation is affixed part of the universe".

Social construction theory is frequently concerned with how our perceptions are influenced by ideas of status and power within a group. Status and power may follow hierarchy or exist along parallel lines in one or more unofficial or tacit understandings of status or power in a group. In religious communities there is often a relationship between perceived adherence and status or privilege.

Beckford writes: "….the status group is often formed out of persons who become committed to the religious practice to a degree that they become standards for the conduct of their entire lives. This gives them a culture and a lifestyle, and also sets of levels of prestige in the surrounding society."

It could be said that that problem with a "we is that it invariably creates a "them." For many people, persons with DD will always be a class apart. We see this often in the infantilization of adults with DD to an extent that is not related to their actual disability. Rapley writes: "…what is to count as (in) competence is negotiated and constructed locally, and for local purposes, by local means. In the case of standardized tests what we have also seen is that the nature of the encouragers required by them produce interactions that are not only shot through with power asymmetry, but also inevitably-in consequence- produce the "impaired' party as 'happy but incompetent'…competence is very much a relative concept, and moreover one which is, in actual social practices, actively negotiated."

Why are we here?

What are the foundations of the current models for inclusion? There are many educational programs for the population and some examples of community. Many of these appear to allow people to "get credit" for doing something for the DD, but that thing isn't inclusion. That is it is not inclusion either into the group or, in a real sense, into the idea set. There is minimal discussion within faiths about how to see beyond the idea of programs and achieve community that involves and blesses all.

Most of the literature on "doing church" is concerned with meeting the requirements of the institution and not the person. To a point this is fair because without some order, the religious institution ceases to be the thing itself. The problem arises when the definition of inclusion is brought to a lowest common denominator that has no reality outside of its application. From this we see the person with DD come into the role of mascot, not member. A person who enters a group having only been asked for "token" engagement may be present, he may even be loved and valued, but the inherent reality of his inclusion is outside himself. It is the difference between the respect accorded an earned degree versus an honorary one.

There are examples of intentional faith communities of persons with DD that address the problem by creating a culture that values engagement over idea sets. One example, the Church of the Exceptional in Rutherfordton, NC, is a self-contained congregation of persons with DD. At the beginning of each service the congregation says a truncated adaptation of a

Christian Creed.

What is remarkable about this is that while the language is truncated, the commitment level required is not. This is important because it establishes the person with DD as having "skin in the game" on a level equal to the requirements of any other faith community using more complex formulas. The active voice, declarative tone of the creed is crucial because it precludes to a great extent the possibility of token membership. Everyone just agreed to the same thing in the same language so no one can be a lesser or greater member of the group. This idea is important to my thesis and will be revisited.

7. The nature of "goals" in inclusion:

Again, as a practical matter, most institutional religions treat persons with DD as a sort of separate caste. Let me repeat, I am in no way suggesting that any particular religious tradition has been remiss per se'. I am suggesting that there has been a tendency to treat DD as a phenomenon somehow "beyond the scope" of the community at large.

There are any number of reasons why this is true, and many of them speak to the social construction of disability. The first is the idea of the person with DD as a problem to be solved. It is to be understood that "What do we DO with so and so?" is a fundamentally different question than "How do we include so and so?" The former implies the institution operating upon the person, the second implies the person operating within the institution. It is the second state of affairs we are after.

With the above in mind, consider the following observation from Luftig regarding the classroom; "Inclusion means more than the child being present for recess and opening exercises, for music and P.E. Children in those placements are just part-time visitors, they do not really belong." (Luftig)

It is worth noting that the operative word here is "belong" not "learn" or "achieve." Even in the educational view, belonging has inherent validity. In a sense all considerations of inclusion of persons with DD into faith communities are considerations of belonging. Even the sort of instruction that most mimics the classroom is only done to facilitate, and make more meaningful, the experience of belonging to the community.

The nature of ritual:

What is a ritual? For the purposes of this discussion, a ritual is any organized behavior that creates identity. That is, a ritual is anything that makes a person self-identify with a group's values and identity, however defined. It need not be an elaborate staged affair along the lines of a high church mass. The complexity of the activity does not a ritual make.

When we discuss inclusion we are ultimately discussing inclusion in ritual behavior irrespective of what that means for any particular faith tradition. The social sciences denote 4 specific things that must be present for a ritual to be meaningful.

As identified by Beckford they are:
1. The physical presence of the person.
2. Barriers to outsiders
3. Mutual focus

4. Shared emotional mood.

These seem simple enough. But what are the practical implications of ideas and how do they translate into real life. One place to start is to deconstruct these ideas in order to see if they lead us to any conclusions.

Physical presence. This seems obvious. A person must be present to be a part of a thing happening in a particular place. Taken a step further, we can extrapolate that their presence must be both voluntary and welcome. It is worth asking: are there degrees of presence? In the case of a person with DD, is the person expected to stay in a physical space reserved for their use? Are they expected to stay on their pew, for example? Is there a relationship between one's place physically in a ritual setting and one's place in the community? Is "sacred space" equally accessible to the person with DD as it is to others? Is access conditional, or is it a function of the needs of the community?

Barriers to outsiders. Most faith communities are to a greater or lesser extent, welcoming of outsiders insofar as general public observances are concerned. For example, as a Christian, I have frequently been a guest in Synagogues and have been treated as a welcome guest (and done my utmost to act as a guest). But my status as an outsider was clear with good reason. The divide between those inside and those outside a community may be hard to quantify in every case but it is real.

No matter how warmly a guest is received they are still a guest. The barriers that exist between insider and outsider in a faith community are typically a function of language. For example, in a traditional Christian setting, the barrier to inclusion in the ritual of Eucharist or communion is affirmation of the belief set of the tradition about what is taking place within the ritual. Likewise, most other faith traditions have similar "lines" that cannot be crossed by people who have not internalized the "truth set" of the tradition.

These barriers are usually contained within the Meta-narrative of the tradition. The relation between the Divine and the group is distinctive- it admits no other equivalent relationship be any other group. Further, it admits no degrees of inclusion. One is either a True believer or some other thing.

This is relevant here because persons with DD are perceived to be unable to either fully understand the nuances of a tradition or to fully invest in a tradition. Neither is universally true. Apart from other factors, most traditions assume a concept of "laity" in which the technical jargon and nuances of a faith tradition's more complex and rarified ideas remain to one degree or another obscure. No one would expect a convert to Christianity to have a working knowledge of biblical Greek as a prerequisite for joining a church, nor would a Jewish congregation expect a gentile to amass a complete understanding of the Torah in Hebrew prior to conversion. The point of this observation is to establish that there exists a precedent for inclusion into most faith communities that is unrelated to intellectual adroitness.

The idea that the ability to retain information and regurgitate it has some connection to one's status within a faith community can be seen as an example of the law of diminishing returns writ large. Clearly, for persons with elevated status -i.e. clergy- there (almost) HAS TO be some relationship between intellectual pursuits and status. But for the rank and file in most traditions, there is a limit on the extent to which intellect equals privilege.

What do we mean by privilege? We mean of course status. In candor, can we assume that in all respects a person DD who is a dependent person in the most essential areas of life is going to be regarded as the "equal" of someone who is successful economically and socially with few impediments? That maybe unrealistic at least as far as our hypothesis goes, at least in terms of the general public perceptions. But we must at least recognize the reality that we will continue to observe a difference between maximum inclusion and a hypothetically perfect inclusion.

What is mutual focus? Mutual focus is the idea that there is both an ultimate reality and a unifying reality that is understood by the group. A "god" is not enough. It must be "our" God as understood by our tradition. There must be a schema that crates the mutual focus. In the context of an inclusion model, this is why mere presence is not enough and group membership is not enough. The person must internalize the Narrative of the group and thus be "oriented" in the same direction as a group in order to be meaningfully included. This is where issues such as coercion and voluntary action becomes important.

We can assume that a person is acting of their own volition but the tendency of persons with DD to anticipate the desired response of a questionnaire and to provide such a response as a survival mechanism and/or habit of life is difficult to overstate.

This is problematic for people who wish to develop a best practice for providing both physical and mental space for people with DD to act as both individuals and as members of a community. Can we assume that mutual focus can mean a common orientation? The difference may be small and semantic, but a "focus" cold be viewed as an emphasis on a problem to be solved or a goal to be reached. An orientation may be simply a tendency to shift one's attention in one direction.

If mutual orientation is understood, rather than mutual focus as understood by the sociological construct, then the ability TO focus on fact sets is removed from the equation. If all of the people in a ritual setting are focusing their minds on 'god' (no matter what that term means in the context of a particular tradition)then the sophistication or lack thereof of any individual community members understand of the fact or the term, is irrelevant to their worth both inherently and as a member of the group.

Put another way, inclusive communities do not privilege classes of laity based on academic knowledge.

Shared emotional mood is another idea that is difficult to quantify. This almost conjures up images of Nuremberg or some sort of Orwellian "hate week." Hopefully nothing of the sort is occurring.

In typical religious settings, what a social scientist means by this could be anything from the generalized good will towards one's fellow man typified by a Unitarian meeting to the ecstasies of a Pentecostal backwoods snake handling meeting.

What is meant is that there is a sense of" we are of a kind, you and I" or of a common cause or ethos. It does not need to mean that everyone is experiencing the exact same level of and specific emotion but that all are sharing what might be termed and "orientation of emotion." That is, all members of the group are experiencing within the parameters of their own temperaments the outcomes of point 3.

Part of the problem in articulating how this 'plays out" for persons with DD is that the larger culture constructs persons with DD as limited in their capacity to understand, control and express their emotions. I say construct because while it is certainly true that some persons with DD do have emotional and behavioral challenges, it is also true that many people who do not have a DD also have difficulty managing their emotions and are not presumed unable to think about or respond to spiritual things as a result.

Many faith traditions have public rituals that are structured to a great degree and admit very little in the way of demonstrative displays of emotion. Others may fall anywhere along a spectrum up to and including traditions that presume enthusiastic, highly emotionally charged responses to be the "authentic" mode of engagement in the tradition.

Without commenting on the legitimacy of any traditions approach to the role of demonstrative emotional response in ritual, these issues do raise some questions for inclusive communities. It is long established that there are tendencies for persons with DD to develop socializing behaviors. That is to say persons with DD are generally speaking understood to seek to blend in with the larger groups with which they associate. A faith community that seeks to maximize inclusion for persons with DD must recognize the potential for demonstrations of emotional mood to be learned approval seeking behavior.

This may be problematic on several levels for the larger community, however, with all due respect to faith traditions, it must be noted (as noted above) that many people present themselves in such a way as to gain approval of the group. We do not presume to know the inner thoughts and possible ulterior motives of all other people. However, in the case of persons with DD there seems to be a sense that it is 'fair game" to speculate on how much they are "getting" out of religious observance. For any number of reasons, I find this offensive.

First, because it implies that religion is about some result (said implication being had with total disregard to the actual values of the tradition, be what they may) that is pre-judged to be beyond the ability of the person with DD to grasp. In this the idea of human transcendence in religion is debased and the implication that the person with DD is either not fully human or a lesser sort is left hanging in the air.

If for example the "point" of religion or of a religion is a transcendent state (getting saved, submitting to the will of Allah, achieving Nirvana, or some other construct) it follows that this transcendent state the normative ideal state as recognized by the tradition. It further follows that as the normative state the ability to enter this state is connected to notions of the humanity of the person seeking the transcendent state.

Bluntly put, to question the sincerity of the emotional responses of persons with DD to religious feeling or to the shared emotional mood of ritual implies a diminished humanity in the question. It would be more appropriate to ask: Does this or that person's emotional response reflect the understandings of the faith tradition?

For example, if a person with DD was smiling or giggling during the very solemn services held on the Christian holiday of Good Friday, this may well be a behavioral problem to be addressed by the person's natural and professional supports. On the other hand, there may be other reasons for the behavior such as simple ignorance of the gravitas of the moment, some unexpected things happening in the room that caught their eye, etc.

This does bring us into a side discussion on the topic of "acquiescence bias." This is the idea, referred to above, that many persons with DD have a tendency to reflexively agree with those with whom they wish to socialize. The phenomenon has been observed to long and so thoroughly that is regarded as an accepted norm of the population. Rapley writes extensive on the topic. He also mentions a corollary idea that is useful to consider at this point. That is the observation that suggestibility, per se' is not an indicator of intelligence, pro or con.

To that end, he quotes Binet at length.

The quote is worth repeating in part because it is so instructive. Binet (as quoted by Rapley) writes: "Suggestibility is by no means a test of intelligence, because very many persons of superior intelligence are susceptible to suggestion, through distraction, timidity, fear of doing wrong, or some preconceived idea. Suggestion produces effects which from certain points of view closely resemble the natural manifestations of feeble-mindedness."

Likewise, someone who is a new convert to a tradition, or is immersed in a varying practice of the same tradition may make a faux pas in the same context. Personally I recall making a minor spectacle of myself in a church of my own tradition on my first visit when I began standing, kneeling and bowing to the rhythm of the service, not realizing that the congregation was using a variation of the ritual with which I was familiar.

The point of this tale is that one need not be a person with DD to attract attention to them-selves in a ritual setting.

Assumptions that all possible variations in affect and behavior in persons with DD in a ritual are a function of their DD make their DD the essence of their personhood. Given that a ritual is supposed to contain these elements, how can we know if it is in some sense successful?

Macionis gives us some indications.

They write:

"If the ritual is successful, four outcomes follow:

A. Group solidarity

B. Symbols representing membership.

C. Emotional energy.

D. Moral standards of right and wrong."

As with the first list, these seem simple enough. They are once again however worth dissecting in order to more fully understand what a new model must accomplish and look like. Group solidarity is not the same thing as "uniformity." It may look more like the solidarity of a family in which people do not need to agree of necessity on every fine point but have a shared sense of community.

This is relevant because while truth-sets and investment in the group meta-narrative are important they are not the sum total of group solidarity. The group itself can be seen to be its own good. Ritual reinforces this, both in placing the individual in relation to the Divine but also in relation to one another. For example, in the communion rite of the Church of Kenya we see the statement, "We are one people, we share one bread."

When we speak of symbols representing membership in a community it is easy to focus on things such as crosses, crescents, and stars which are literal physical objects that identify the person wearing or displaying them as members of a group. These things are surely symbols of membership.

However, this phenomenon works on two levels. Beyond tokens we see that symbols of membership can also include behaviors engaged in or directed towards a person so as to indicate membership. Most ritual activities do not directly use physical symbols as such but use symbolic behavior. While for the most part, this conduct is directed towards completion of the ritual itself, much symbolic behavior is engaged in within group of people during ritual observance. An obvious example would be the "secret handshake" used by some fraternal organizations.

For the purpose of our discussion we can consider such behaviors as the joining of hands for group prayer or the exchange of "the peace." These are behaviors that are part and parcel of the ritual but are also intended to signify that one member is affirming the "rightness" of another member in this place. Emotional energy is an idea that can mean many things. It is not of necessity the same thing as the idea of a shared emotional mood noted above. It could be more readily understood as the outgrowth of such a mood. Emotional energy may be "excitement" could it not also describe the commitment to an ideal that is embodied in service to others?

If emotional energy is that which denotes a state of mind that is engaged and not passive, than quiet contemplation may well be directed emotional energy just as much as more observable demonstrative conduct.

The idea of moral standards of right and wrong are easy to codify but difficult to contextualize. Assuming for a moment that a community's notion of right or wrong fall somewhere within the general cultural norms we may be tempted to ask ourselves: Do not most people with DD have natural and professional supports concerned with matters of conduct? Does the community have a responsibility to a behavior plan? This may have some almost cynical, pragmatic logic of a kind but it shows an understanding of inclusion that is 180 degrees out of phase with our model.

Regardless of what we may remember from childhood brushes with authority, moral standards are not properly the control mechanisms of privilege. They are those things which the group says about right conduct insofar as the individual relates to the corporate and its various members. They say in part that a member of the community believes thus and so about whence the morality came. Further, because the authority for the morals is accepted as privileged, the group may publish moral teachings it is proper for the member to adhere to as a response to the pull of membership.

If the first step in belonging is to say "we believe this," then the next logical step is to say; "We do or do not do a thing as an identifier of membership in the community who believe the above." It is worth noting that the implied corollary to moral standards is a prerogative to enforce them.

Do faith communities have either a right or an obligation to enforce morality on persons with DD? To some extent the answer has to be yes, at least so far as behavior posing grave danger is concerned. Beyond that, it is worth remembering that our goal is an inclusion for persons with DD that is inherently beyond the status of a "mascot" for the community. It stands to reason that meaningful inclusion will involve, indeed must involve, moments of growth, reflection and correction; just as it does for everyone else.

This does bring us to a brief discussion of behavior. Behavior per se' has very little to do with morals and ethics and a great deal to do with the mores of the culture attempting to mitigate a behavior. A behavior may obviously be moral but not appropriate or in no way impolite but morally offensive. It is worth noting here that behaviors that are part of disease pathology are not really under the purview of a faith community except to maintain order and decorum.

It is reasonable to assume that from time to time persons with DD, having become integrated into the community may offend a person or rule so as to bring notice upon themselves. Put another way, everybody gets someone's attention eventually. In my case it usually involves parking tickets. We must disabuse ourselves of the notion that to have expectations of persons with DD is to place them in an artificially subordinate position. It is not, as long as the relationship between the person and the authority in the community is what it would be in the absence of DD.

We can, and do, rearrange public spaces to make accommodations; not just to the building but to our minds. A narrative model is going to be less concerned with rules than values. This is done with the understanding that morals are extrapolated from the meta-narrative of a faith community, not that which constructs the community. This makes the person responsible for the morals of the group not beholden to them. The reinforcement of morals should be an internalization of the morals not a reminder to comply with them.

8. DRAWING CONCLUSIONS: How is Inclusion currently done?

There are varied approaches to inclusion in the religious landscape. To begin with one example, in the Roman Catholic tradition, the participation in the Mass is denoted as of great importance. Much of the overall inclusion model therein is thus focused on preparing the individual with DD for participation in this ritual. This is evident when reviewing the SPREAD program literature.

The SPREAD program is a curriculum intended to prepare developmentally disabled persons to be involved in the Mass. It is the primary Special education population curriculum for Roman Catholics in the US. A neutral observer could easily, and mistakenly, infer from the curriculum that learning-by-rote the necessary behaviors to get from the beginning to the end in the Mass is the thing itself, and that once the person with DD has successfully passed this milestone, they are on their own.

However, it must be stated that the guidelines for worship in the Roman Catholic Church are adamant that the person with DD is in every sense a member of the community. I mention this at the outset of this discussion because in my own encounters with Catholic laity who were charged with supporting persons with

DD I was aware of a deep commitment to transcending the conventional public worship model to arrive at a place in which the necessity of inclusion in "parish life" is the ultimate goal.

The current models and their pros and cons:

This does provide us with a perfect segue into a larger and more meaningful question. What does inclusion mean? Re-stated so as to get to the heart of the matter, beyond the right to be present, what does inclusion mean? I would submit there is no "right" answer. But the question is instructive in that it would allow for a full and complete inclusion model to be demonstrated.

This brings up an important distinction in that most of the religious traditions that have tackled this issue at the institutional level have affirmed the individual in some metaphysical sense. Obviously, this paper cannot address all of the possible theological implications of, and theories about, disability. There are some assumptions that are as nearly universal as to be applicable. The first is the inherent humanity of the individual. The ability of the person with DD to make meaningful choices is almost universally recognized. The notion of degrees of DD is recognized widely but (I believe) receives short shrift in most of the literature. Lastly, (and not discussed nearly enough) the ability of persons with DD to "sense" or commune with the

Metaphysical Other as defined by the faith tradition.

A new paradigm:

Having deconstructed the elements of ritual in the context of their application in developing an inclusive community, can we draw any conclusions? The central idea of this thesis is that we can draw inferences and conclusions about how to best develop models for including persons with DD into faith communities from an examination of the literature on special education, the relevant social sciences and the relevant literature on religion and practice.

With that in mind, it is worth remembering that this thesis began with the request to develop a model for including persons with DD into a local congregation. The research above does provide point towards some general conclusions which can be synthesized below. This is essentially what has been learned.

An interactive, narrative based ritual model for persons with Developmental Disabilities

To return to the question we began with, what are the current best practices? There are several examples of religious education and inclusion for persons with DD. The above mentioned

SPREAD program developed by the Roman Catholic Church is a good case study in the state of the art.

It is essentially a program of catechesis developed for the DD population and is intended in large measure to prepare the person to receive the sacraments of the church. Since this act is the central defining act of membership in the tradition, this is reasonable. This program goes to great lengths to use sensitive language, is fully invested in the current state of DD educational research, and is in every way an impressive example of the faith tradition reaching out to the DD population.

Most of the institutional religious bodies have something similar in intent if not in content. However, the underlying assumption (here and elsewhere) is that the way to do inclusion is to take what works in the Special Ed classroom or the Sheltered Workshop and apply the methodology to the faith.

Since there was really no where else to turn for models for so long, this is reasonable. However, over the past few years a body of literature has arisen which gives us insight into how to look at the issue beyond the scope of the classroom. We have the ability to rethink inclusion based on new data.

It may be beneficial to begin looking at the problem by asking some questions. Questions like:

Does the person with DD perceive a difference in them-selves or, is it socially constructed?

How does the person with DD experience religion outside of the actual inclusion event (religious service or other group activity)?

Does DD change the ability of the person to "process" metaphysics? That is, is the ability to experience religious feeling or devotion a function of intelligence?

Does social and emotional maturity play a role in how persons with DD engage with the conflicts and complexities of religious life?

What does it mean to "believe" in something, when your cognitive abilities are suspect? What are the implications of conflict between traditions and the ideas of "exclusivity" inherent in many traditions in the lives of people socialized to avoid conflict (as many persons with DD are)?

What are the faith traditions responsibilities to the person? Do they include moral accountability?

How does a faith tradition consider the issue of voluntary conduct, versus disease pathology, in the case of someone with, say, Tourette's syndrome or another behavior disorder?

How does it deal with the issues inherent in group discipline?

How does it deal with the potential implications of cognitive disability and heresy?

One response to all of the above is to consider a mindset rather than deciding on a policy. There is always much discussion of "behavior" when considering inclusion of persons with DD in to "mainstream" social settings. At the risk of self contradiction, I am reminded that we are ultimately considering how to achieve "maximum" inclusion not hypothetically idealized inclusion.

The following observation from Koegel is insightful Koegel writes: "The wider the latitude available for modifying the life arrangements for a person with challenging behaviors, the less precise and technical behavior programming needs to be."

The point here being that if we create an environment that is truly safe and meaningful, much of the endlessly discussed cycle of behavioral triggers and accommodations that is part of the daily life of the natural and professional supports of persons with DD may resolve itself to some degree.

This is not to suggest that specific definitive answers to any of all of the above are part of this essay or even necessary in another context. The point is to make plain how complex the issues really are. It is easy to assume that any interaction with persons with DD is going to be both simple and paternalistic. This is not the case. I am not suggesting that a model of inclusion will suddenly answer every question and resolve every conflict in the life of a faith community that is inclusive of persons with MR.

I would however submit that (for one) we have to start somewhere and (for another) the place to start is the actual mechanics of communication.

9. A new model for inclusion:

There have been a variety of attempts to develop a program of public religious observance for the use of the developmentally disabled. This is laudable. However, it does stand to reason that a better model would be a practice of public group religious observance that is meaningful to the widest possible spectrum of persons.

That is to say, if persons with DD are indeed members of a faith community in a meaningful sense, then the actual act of participation- the ritual, service, or by any other name, ought to both reflect this truth and pronounce this truth.

Education: How can we best apply the paradigm to religious instruction?

Much has been done in this area and it is easy to imagine much will continue to be done. Some points of personal pique do come to mind. If I accomplish nothing by writing this paper than to convince leaders of DD ministries in local congregations to stop using terms like "our special friends" or "our special buddies." or similar demeaning monikers, I will see this as time well spent. Frankly, I would imagine that any of the commercially available curriculums for religious instruction for persons with DD are admitting any number of caveats) are as good as any other as far as they go.

If the intent is to provide a set of facts that defines the group then as long as those fact sets are delineated in a way that is meaningful, then this model can at best "tweak" the language of any one program to make it fit more narrative driven or what have you. The point of the model is context, not textbook writing. If information is presented in a way that manifests inclusion as opposed to describing inclusion then it has done the thing we are driving for.

Allow me a deliberately ham-fisted example of what I mean; consider the following 2 statements: 1. "It is my duty as a member of this church, in accordance with the doctrines set forth and codified at our last quarterly meeting, to uphold a statement that God is love and that as such love is a requirement for fellowship in this body, as incorporated under the articles of our charter, and that forthwith this applies to all parties described as members under said articles." 2. "I love you." The first is an idea. The second is a STORY. It is a story that engages the soul and mind of the teller and the hearer.

This is the thing that all of the technical jargon of the academic literature tells us is missing from the current models of instruction and inclusion. Our ancient ancestors were much more comfortable with the notion of myth (in the sense of a "narrative that explains the facts") not because they were ignorant but because an auditory (that is to say narrative driven) culture understands that narrative provides schema. It makes the pieces fit.

No amount of reading my wife's medical records or pouring over her resume' for example, is going to make me love her and want to raise children with her. I first had to become invested in the story: who is this person and what makes them tick, before the data sets became relevant. And, this is important, it is unlikely I would have been able to extrapolate the story from the data, no matter how it was presented. I had to hear the story and see myself as a part of the story before investing in the community (in this case, a community of 2 adults, one school age child, a toddler, 2 fish and a hermit crab). It is also worth noting that structured, ritualized activities facilitated this process. These rituals involved shared meals, rote dialogue, candles, and many of the other tropes of religious ritual.

In the same sense that we use this narrative driven ritual activity to build inclusive 2 person communities, we use the same tools to build larger ones. It is tempting to delve into the technical literature and to make a case for a series of recommendations intended to tweak any one of the existing curricula for religious instruction for persons with DD.

The main novel idea of this book as it applies to education and instruction, is the use of the narrative as the essential tool for both communicating information and for communicating inclusion. With this in mind, the specific examples altering existing models or promoting new ones are not done for the sake of the specific ideas themselves, but to demonstrate their utility in the contexts in which they are presented.

Ritual: "How do we "make it happen?"

There can perhaps be any number of ways to facilitate this. There is one example of a type that does suggest itself is an interactive form known as a Litany. For the purpose of this discussion it is best considered as an example-of-a-type. That is, it is a pattern or type of ritual observance that has a history of being inclusive of and bringing together diverse groups of people. And so, is useful as a basis for demonstrating how the model could be applied within faith traditions.

The Litany motif is one of the oldest forms of public religious observance. Essentially the term refers to any of a number of interactive rituals in which a person in leadership leads the group through a "call and response." The cleric makes statements, typically in praise of, or describing the merits of, the Deity and the group responds with one or more rote response either of assent or corollary statements.

This process is repeated until the statements relevant to that specific ritual event have all been articulated. The general form has precedent in a variety of cultures and religions. The form most commonly known as a litany has its origins in the public observance of ancient Judaism and early Christianity, and the essential forms have long been noted in virtually every religion of the east and west.

What is relevant for our purposes is that the Litany was a very common form of group ritual activity in pre-literate societies. A brief glance at an example of litany may suggest some clues as to its usefulness in creating inclusion.

For example, the passage below is a fragment of the litany of the Saints as outlined by Maeesy:

Clergy: O God the Father of heaven.
Response: Have mercy upon us.
Clergy: O God the Son, Redeemer of the world.
Response: Have mercy upon us.

Other than the obvious distinction between clergy and laity the actual process of a litany has the effect of creating a certain leveling in status among and between participants. Most of the language used is in the personal plural. The language says "we believe, we affirm, we speak with one voice": these are the messages of a litany.

Litany (and in the broader sense liturgy) is not in the main a private, personalized activity. It is a team sport; however , no one is any better or worse at it. By agreeing together to a series of statements the community joins themselves to the formational narrative of the community. The group becomes "the people who believe thus and so." Since all have affirmed, all are in equal standing in the shared belief set.

Largely apart from the issue of disability, a litany transcends the wide variety of barriers to inclusion and companionship that are common in most social interactions. One does not have to be well educated or articulate to participate. The fact set laid out in a litany is already understood to be "core knowledge" of the communities' beliefs. It could be assumed reasonably that whatever soul searching the individual participant needed to do had been done well beforehand. Thus it lends itself to the individual becoming immersed in the activity.

The responses of a litany are easily learned and if not learned by rote is, by the nature of the process, prompted. Many examples of litany and related liturgical rituals for use by persons of either limited educational or functional language ability exist. For example in some parts of the emerging world where local and tribal languages predominate, a litany in a common, ostensibly neutral language may serve to bind persons of dispirit backgrounds into a common community.

Much the same thing is intended here. I submit that a common ritual observance based on the forms of a litany has potential to offer a maximum of inclusion into the mainstream of faith communities to persons with DD.

Note here again; for the purposes of this work, this paper is making my case for solely for the applicability of the model. There is no intent to promote any theological idea of any kind. The evidence has pointed me towards seeking a model for inclusion that is egalitarian, interactive, and capable of meeting the emotional needs of the community. The case is being made here that a litany is a useful example of an existing ritual model that has the benefit of being highly suited to meeting the needs of faith communities that seek to maximize inclusion of persons with DD into their public observances. Secondly, a description of a model for public observance that constitutes evidence based practice serves another role. It supports the idea that the full body of evidence for a variety of disciplines can be brought to bear on questions of inclusion.

Regardless of the applicability of this specific example of evidence based model may be to any person or situation process of moving beyond the domains of education and behavior management remains a useful paradigm in developing inclusion models for any number of communities. The ideas would apply to inclusion in social clubs, fraternal organizations (ostensibly of the Moose Lodge variety, not the Animal House kind though, I don't see any reason why not) social service organizations, organizations based on common identity such as ethnic, cultural, or any other identity.

In practice, a litany for public worship to be used by integrated (DD and non-DD) would be built around common themes that reinforce the ethos of the group. The questions "Who are we, and why are we here?" would be asked and answered. The answer would be essentially: "We are the people who believe these things and we are here to make manifest our common identity." To many minds the idea of responsive verbalization conjures up images of mindless repetition or coerced behavior.

The particular dangers of ritualized behavior as they relate to "acquiescence bias" will not be delved into again except to say that one point of rote repetition of language in ritual is to get the mind beyond the focus on the immediate academic understanding of the language to foster a group ethos.

Also, the idea is not to develop a plan resembling a lesson plan. The idea is to realize our values. In fact, a specific one-size-fits-all plan is not beneficial. It is likely to invoke the law of unintended externalities. That is, the idea that every time you do something to solve a problem, you create the potential for a new problem.

Put another way, this book is an attempt to replace a love rules with a rule of love.

A place at the table: A handbook for facilitators of inclusive worship.

As a way of demonstrating the application of this thesis, I have prepared a brief guide for inclusive services for persons with DD. It is essentially the document I was asked to prepare when this process started. I have taken the considerable liberty of preparing it according to its original intent. That is, I do not shy away from religious language in this section as it is only meaningful as a guide if such language is included. I have every reason to assume that the academic work on which it is based is transferable to any other faith tradition.

Permission is given to faith communities to copy the manual section below for administrative/educational use.

Introduction-Why should Christians CARE about doing church for the Developmentally Disabled?

One of the things I find most disturbing about so many of the conversations I have had on the topic of "why" do we do religious observance involving persons with DD is that so many of the conversations devolve to questions about the metaphysics of the soul of the person with DD and questions about the relationship between reasoning ability and sin; or even questions about the propriety of allowing persons with DD in the church and the like. These questions are offensive on many a level, but there is a central tenet of the Christian faith that is either not understood or willfully ignored by the above described questioner: Humans are here to worship God. That is the point of being alive. It is what we are made for and made to do. The poet William Blake called us "God's machineries of Joy" for good reason. We bring goodness, holiness, into the world through our prayers and praises. The act of worship, of recognizing God for who he is, makes us what we are. The praises of the people of God, "of all sorts and conditions of man" as the prayer book says, are beautiful to the ears of the faithful and to God.

That a child of God has unique challenges or is limited in some capacity in no way diminishes this truth. Ultimately, all of the thought and attention paid to programs and methodologies for stage managing church services so as to make them conducive to participation by persons with DD can be summed up in the proposition that we are merely providing a time and space for these people to do that which they were born to do, as were all of us. There is nothing of greater importance than the act of praising God and of offering worship. To provide a place for people who have been marginalized to come and worship as "fellow citizens" is a noble task and one that allows the Holy Spirit to work in and through those who travel with persons with

DD on the journey of life.

To those who would focus on the challenges inherent in such an undertaking I would suggest that compared to the petty snits and quarrels of any other human community the difficulties arising in providing a place at the table of the Family of God for persons with DD are small indeed. When the soul of any one of us is in adoration of our God, heaven is touched and the Kingdom is within us. The ground upon which they stand is holy. The notion that a deviation in a score on a Stanford-Binet intelligence test somehow alters these fundamental truths is outrageous.

Yet, people continue to ask: "Isn't God just going to be kind to people 'like that' anyway? Why do we need to get involved? I don't think God would send them to hell so what does it matter?" These sorts of questions do not deserve a response except to say that it is a strange sort of religion that looks at reaching out in love to other people through a sort of cost-benefit analysis. The praises of God's people do not need any justification. We were born to be loved and to love in return. All who share in this truth must know that bringing it to others is our calling. Faith comes by hearing.

The research on which this hand book is based supports the idea that a narrative-driven approach to inclusion is preferable. By narrative-driven it is meant that the story of faith and the person's place within that story are the guiding ideas. The intent is to move away from programs of ministry to persons with DD that are focused on controlling behavior or on teaching rote behaviors so as to allow token participation in group activities.

That is the hope is to engage the imagination of people with DD so as to make inclusion as natural and as meaningful as possible.

WHO, WHAT, WHERE, WHEN, AND WHY: The mechanics of an inclusive service.

WHO: Who are the persons a particular service is intended to reach?

The actual specifics will be different from location to location. It is important however to consider that the idea here is not to just re-imagine MR/DD ministry.

Properly understood, any service of public worship is open to all, an inclusive service is merely adapted to the needs of those present. This is not to say that the necessary adaptation does not require forethought. Persons involved in ministry (hereafter referred generically as "ministers" regardless of clerical title) to persons with DD ought to have a personal relationship with the people in their local congregation they are attempting to serve. It is also appropriate (with due respect paid to privacy concerns) that they have some understanding of the actual conditions of each individual in much the same way that any other minister would make an effort to know their congregation.

For example; if the ministry is including persons with serious physical limitations who are not cognitively impaired, into a service designed for persons with limited intellectual functioning, there may be an opportunity to expand the ministry.

Note that there is no suggestion that the approach is wrong or that anyone is being insensitive. The idea here is that an inclusive worship service is not about creating new, or more politically correct, pigeonholes. It is about engaging with people in ways that are meaningful. Persons ministering to the DD population should be willing to develop an understanding of the specific challenges faced by their flock.

Ministers need to be willing to act in concert with the natural and professional supports that are already in place for the person. For example, this may mean that ministers may have to reach understandings about sharing information regarding behavior or be willing to work within pre-existing behavior plans.

Part of truly loving others is being a teller of the truth. It may be that serving some persons in an adaptation of public worship is beyond the abilities of a particular congregation at a particular point in time. The building may not be suitable for whatever reason and it may be that a congregation may not have the personnel or skill sets to assist persons with specific behavioral or physical challenges. If this is the case, it is better to admit it and find either the resources or alternatives to properly serve the person.

It does no good to make the people involved in a ministry feel better about them-selves for including someone if doing so places the person or others in harm's way.

WHAT. What does an inclusive Church Service look like?

Clearly there is going to be substantial variation from congregation to congregation. However, the evidence from the educational sphere would tend to support a high degree of structure. This does not mean a sort-of precision drill exercise.

By structure, we mean both that the service itself is predictable and that the environment is consistent and stable. A good example would be using the same physical space routinely. Having services at consistent times of the day and week is another important part of building structure. Having an order of service is important, as it defines exactly what is happening and what the person is being included in to. Also, if a service is predictable it may actually reduce distraction and inattention, as knowing where one is in a service is part of feeling engaged in it. Most congregations have an existing rubric that is adaptable.

A clear beginning, middle and end are important for fostering engagement. Most churches use (or recognize as legitimate) some form of public group prayer or other statement. These can include creeds, responsive readings, litanies, and so on. These types of activities are very useful in inclusive worship services and are meaningful both as worship and in building community.

There are many examples available of public responsive worship developed for and easily adapted to, persons with DD. It is worth noting that group activities of this type both tell a story, and inherently are a story. Such things as the use of the personal plural (us, we, our) language engage the worshipper. Sermons and teaching do not necessarily have to be lectures by authority figures but can utilize parable, and other literary devices to engage the listener.

Involving congregants in reading scripture or in sharing from their lives engages the person and the listener on many levels. Extemporaneous prayer allows people to engage both vertically with God and horizontally with those who pray with them. Inclusion can take many forms but it should be about engagement with and immersion in the "Meta-Narrative"-the story the community tells itself about itself. It should say, "We belong here", not just "we attend an activity here."

Lastly, some care should be taken to ensure that persons who do not have DD are welcome. The idea is to create new space, not separate space, in the church. The families, caregivers, professional support and others who attend should know that they are welcomed and valued for their presence not merely for their function.

A note on education: There are an astonishing number of programs, workbooks, guides; etc for implementing religious education in individuals with DD. Almost any of them will do, provided they support the values and beliefs of the church using them. Having said that, care should be taken in selecting a program as most of them are what may be termed "fact driven."

That is, their emphasis is on learning sets of facts with little context. Facts matter. It is important to know the ideas and beliefs of one's church. But, especially for persons with DD, fact sets with out a narrative context can easily become trivia. It may be useful to edit or modify whatever program is used to emphasize context over rote memorization.

If at all possible, it is advisable to have someone with a background in Special Education overseeing religious education as a separate thing apart from worship, and other group activities. Religious education is important. However, all too often it has been seen as the point, and the only point of engagement by churches and persons with DD. If we are not creating a space where persons with DD can worship, what possible good does en educational program in religion do?

WHERE: Where do we do inclusive services?

This question is ultimately going to be answered by the local church according to the realities of their buildings and other resources. There are some values however that should be taken into account to the greatest extent possible. It is important to ensure that the actual location of a service is both practical and meaningful. If at all possible, an inclusive service would be held in the place of inclusion- the primary worship space of the congregation. Ideally, all persons with DD who can attend "regular" (someday we'll find a better term) services ought to do so, and accommodations can be made in a great many cases.

Persons ministering to the DD population should recognize that attending services should not be an either/or proposition and careful to avoid the notion that one is for this group of persons and one is for another group. Depending on the size of the group and the resources available it may be necessary to "do" worship at a time when the primary worship space is in use.

There is no wrong place per se' but it is productive to select a space that is comfortable, not noisy or used for other things and does not suggest marginalization by its location. To cite an actual example, in the basement behind the boiler room may not be the best choice. Again, we are including people into the story of our congregations.

The location of the space used does say something about the status of the people using the space. The consideration of location does bring up some related issues. It is important to know your congregation's needs and preferences when selecting and modifying space. Unusual and loud noises, harsh or unusual lighting and jarring or distracting imagery may be behavioral triggers in many persons with behavioral and perceptual difficulties.

Physical access is an important consideration in selecting a location. Many older church buildings do not have accessible architecture and may have inadequate bathroom facilities to accommodate some disabilities. Accommodations developed to assist one population may not benefit another. For example, the ramped curbs designed to facilitate wheelchair use are very dangerous to persons with vision impairments. Talk to your local fire marshal about local regulations. They may also be able to advise you on how best to use your space. Talk to the congregation and their natural and professional supports to get some idea as to the needs of your local group.

When. In a perfect world, all persons regardless of disability would be able to join together in corporate worship.

In reality, it is often beneficial to develop the sorts of environments we are discussing here. What is important is that an ethos be defined that says that we develop worship opportunities for persons with DD that draw them towards the center of the group rather than push them to the margins. The differences may be subtle but they are real. In the case of scheduling it is once again important to communicate with the congregation. Many persons with DD live in group homes or other intentional communities. Many have work and educational schedules. In short, they live normal lives.

Engaging the persons and their supports may provide insight into what will work best for your group. The scheduling of your service also says a lot about the importance of you service to the larger community. Is it at a time when the building is being used for other activities? Are these uses seen as competitive or complementary? Is the service scheduled in such a way as to encourage the perception that this service is part of the normal rhythm of the life of the congregation? Can it be scheduled so as to allow interaction with other groups using the space that is a benefit to all? Are there conflicts that need to be preempted?

Some general rules of thumb may be helpful.

Most "day-programs" are finished by 3pm or so in order to allow for transportation to be completed in a timely manner. Most group homes and facilities have transportation services that prefer to run earlier rather than later. Unless your church is directly on a special needs bus line (a very rare occurrence) you will either have to provide transportation (very expensive) or schedule your services to accommodate whatever transportation realities you encounter. You will need to determine what your church liability insurance carrier says about transportation issues as well. For some reason, Tuesday and Thursdays evenings have become popular times to schedule religious services for persons with DD. The only reason that comes to mind is that these times would likely be agreeable to residential staff. The real issue is whether the persons with DD are meaningfully engaged. Does the time set aside for demonstrate that they are part of our story

WHY: Christians refer to the defining narrative of their religion as the gospel- the good news.

At the core of Christianity (and indeed all religions) is a story. We believe that this story applies to all people in all circumstances. Everything that is done or not done to include persons with DD into the daily life of a church must reflect a belief in the inherent worth of the individual with DD in the eyes of God and in the eyes of the Church. They are part of THE story and part of OUR story. No amount of program development can displace real human engagement.

Engagement means exactly what it means for persons without a DD diagnosis; a commitment to the person as a brother or sister. People with DD face the same moral and spiritual challenges as everyone else. They will disappoint us. Just as we all disappoint those we love. They will also inspire us, just was we seek to bring out the best in others. These are the realities of being human. The whole point of this handbook is that people with DD are fully and completely human. If you keep that in mind, your program will succeed.

It may seem like straining at gnats to differentiate between a sense of pity and a sense of injustice, but it is vital. A desire to implement meaningful opportunities for persons with DD to worship that are born out of a desire to right a wrong (kept in check by prudence) is a gift from God. A desire to do something, anything really, out of a sense of pity may be morally right and sincere but it will invariably lead to a sort of benign contempt. Worship is simply too important to be sullied with such.

Lastly, the reason that doing all of these things matters is that if the story, the gospel is true than it is true for all mankind. The gospel is central both to our motivation and to its implementation. The story is for everyone. The story is about everyone. If we begin with that truth, everything else we do will fall into place.

Affirmations for providers of services and support of inclusion for persons with disabilities and other special life circumstances:

1. We affirm that all people are made in the image of God and that our faith calls us to respond to "all sorts and conditions of men."

We affirm that people are not their circumstances, and that people are not problems to be solved. In this we affirm that persons with disabilities are not in our community to be corrected, set right, or repaired as concerns their disability.

3. We affirm that full acceptance of a person includes accountability to the communities' ethics and values; as to do otherwise is to relegate them to a second class status within our community. In this we offer encouragement, not capricious judgment. We affirm that forbearance will never become the "soft bigotry of lowered expectations."

4. We affirm that any who bless us with their presence in good will are a blessing to us all. In this, we affirm the work of the Holy Spirit in the lives of the disabled. We likewise affirm the work of the Holy Spirit throughout our community through the lives and examples of persons with disabilities.

5. We affirm that God is glorified by the praises of all of his people. A statement of operational ethics and best practice for inclusive communities and programs intended for the benefit of persons with DD.

As confirmation that we understand the gravity of the of the trust imparted to us by persons with DD and their natural and professional supports, we agree that we do not practice psychotherapy (by whatever term) unless formally trained and licensed to do so by the state. We listen, we love, we pray, and we encourage, but we do not practice medicine.

We admit when we are unable to help a specific individual with either short or long term needs, and will do all in our power to secure the proper help. We affirm in all ways the power of prayer and the ministry of the Holy Spirit. Because of our sure knowledge of this ministry, we will not at any time divert or redirect a person away from the support of the medical, mental health, substance abuse disciplines and/or other supports.

We promise to communicate fully and candidly with church leadership and authorities when responding to a crisis. We accept that a person's true circumstances may not be fully known to us. We accept that simple goodwill does not qualify us to be all things to all people.

In this we pledge to work with interdisciplinary teams- natural and professional supports- that offer support to the persons with DD we encounter. We agree to the proper and right use of boundaries, personal, ethical and moral, in offering aid to others. We affirm that we are called to a work of service, not self-fulfillment. We accept that what makes us feel good may not be in another's best interest. We accept we may never hear the words "thank you."

Permission is granted to print this section for use in training materials.

BIBLIOGRAPHY:

Beckford, James A. Ed. The Sage Handbook of religions.
London: SAGE Publications, 2007. Print

Diaz, Carlos F. Multicultural education for the 21sr Century. New York: Addison-WesleyLongman, 2001 Print

Rapley, Mark.The Social Construction of Intellectual Disability. Cambridge UK: Cambridge University Press, 2004.

Florian, L. The Sage Handbook of Special Education.London: Sage Publications, 2007. Print.

Hattum, Rolland. Developmental Language programming for the Retarded. London:Allyn and Bacon 1979

Macionis, John. Sociology. New York: Prentice Hall, 2007.

Luftig, Richard. Teaching the Mentally Retarded Student. London: Allyn & Bacon , 1987.

Koegel, L. K., Kogel, R. L., & Dunlap, G. Positive behavioral support: Including people with difficult behavior in the Community.Baltimore: Paul Brookes Publishing Co.

Shepard, Maeesy. The Oxford American Prayer Book Commentary. New York: Oxford University Press, 1950 ISBN-13: 978-1492185796 ISBN-10: 1492185795

Printed in Great Britain
by Amazon